BEHIND
THE
SCENES

Bouncing off the Menu

Also in the same series:

The Wildlife Games

An Island Escape

A Guest Appearance

Dive in Deeper

A Ghostly Tale

BEHIND THE SCENES

Bouncing off the Menu

Written by Jess Black

RANDOM HOUSE AUSTRALIA

A Random House book
Published by Random House Australia Pty Ltd
Level 3, 100 Pacific Highway, North Sydney NSW 2060
www.randomhouse.com.au

First published by Random House Australia in 2012

Addresses for companies within the Random House Group can be found at
www.randomhouse.com.au/offices.

National Library of Australia
Cataloguing-in-Publication Entry

Author: Irwin, Bindi, 1998–
Title: Bindi Behind the Scenes: Bouncing off the Menu /
Bindi Irwin, Jess Black
ISBN: 978 1 86471 843 0 (pbk)
Series: Irwin, Bindi, 1998– Bindi behind the scenes; 5.
Target audience: For primary school age
Other authors/contributors: Black, Jess
Dewey number: A823.4

Cover photograph © Australia Zoo
Cover and internal design by Christabella Designs
Typeset by Midland Typesetters, Australia
Printed in Australia by Griffin Press, an accredited ISO AS/NZS
14001:2004 Environmental Management System printer

Random House Australia uses papers that are natural, renewable and
recyclable products and made from wood grown in sustainable forests.
The logging and manufacturing processes are expected to conform to the
environmental regulations of the country of origin.

Dear Diary,

My family love to show off our beautiful country, so when some old family friends said they were visiting Australia for the first time, we wanted to WOW them! We planned a train trip to the Red Centre of the outback to explore Uluru and see some wildlife. But it turned out that kangaroos were more likely to be seen on a restaurant menu than in the wild!

While visiting a kangaroo rescue centre in Alice Springs, my friend Damian and I were invited on an outback adventure to release a rescued kangaroo back into the wild. We learnt about the cruel practices used to cull kangaroos and the threat of kangaroos becoming endangered in some parts of Australia.

Like me, my friends Damian and Len had both experienced the death of a loved one at an early age. Damian was struggling to come to terms with his grief and needed our help. His journey reminded me of life lesson number five:

A journey of a thousand miles begins with a single step.

Little did we know that we would soon be put to the test when we came face to face with a roo hunter who threatened everything Len holds dear.

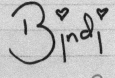

CHAPTER ONE

BINDI GAVE HER ARMS A BIG stretch as her distance education studies were finally coming to an end for the day. Her shoulders felt cramped after hours of maths and she was sure she had a mild, if not moderate, case of brain drain.

Bindi and her teacher, Sarah, were grappling

with one last maths equation. Bindi stared at the maths formula on page twenty-five of her textbook, but the letters and numbers seemed to blur together the longer she looked at it.

'What is the value of the formula when D equals 5?' repeated Sarah. She looked up from the textbook and, taking note of Bindi's blank look, laughed. 'Okay, enough for today but I want you to work on the answer as homework. Go on then, get out of here!'

Bindi couldn't pack up her books fast enough. While she liked learning, Bindi also enjoyed the outdoors. It was a beautiful and sunny Queensland day, and Bindi wanted to make the most of the daylight hours she had left.

'Thanks, Sarah!' Bindi called as she made her

way out of the office they used as a schoolroom at Australia Zoo. 'See you tomorrow!'

Bindi smiled as she felt the warmth of the sun on her face. Most kids had to travel to and from school but her home and school were in the same place. She was also lucky enough to have hundreds of exotic and Australian animals at her doorstep! Living in a zoo meant that Bindi had no shortage of human *and* animal friends to keep her company. In fact, it was almost a full-time job making sure she kept up with all that was going on with her animal friends.

Bindi ran through the list in her head, trying to prioritise who to visit first. She knew Alimah the albino Burmese python always enjoyed a visit, and that Geraldine the giraffe was close to giving birth. But Bindi had also heard news that there had been a new arrival in the red panda enclosure that morning, and that baby Clara was causing quite a stir.

'Hi Henry!' Bindi called to a sturdy wombat that was out for a waddle with his keeper. Seeing Henry gave Bindi an idea. She hadn't visited the koala and kangaroo enclosure lately, and she had a soft spot for a certain mother and son. Her mind was made up about how best to spend the next few hours.

Thinking that she should check in with her mum first, Bindi rummaged through her backpack and pulled out a walkie-talkie. She tuned it to the private frequency she and her mum could use. For some families, communicating by walkie-talkie might seem like a novelty, but for the Irwins it was as common as texting or calling by phone. It was just another way of keeping in touch!

'Hi Mum. Over!' Bindi spoke into the radio.

There was a crackle followed by a short pause before her mother's voice could be heard. 'Hey sweetheart, how was school? Over.'

'Algebra and I had a wrestle, and I'm not yet sure who won. Over,' replied Bindi.

'Say no more!' laughed Terri. 'Over.'

'I'm going to head over to see Tommy and Pebbles, is that okay? Over,' said Bindi, as she zigzagged her way past a family of five who had stopped to admire the photo board.

'No problem. Just be home in time for dinner. Over,' said Terri. Bindi was about to turn off her walkie-talkie when her mum's voice crackled through the static again. 'Actually, can you swing past and pick up Robert? I think he could do with some fresh air. Over.'

Bindi grinned. That was her mum's diplomatic way of saying that Robert was climbing the walls and was probably enjoying her fourth meeting for the day about as much as Bindi relished algebra.

'Be there in a jiffy. Over,' Bindi replied, and broke into a jog. It felt good to use her muscles after hours of sitting behind a desk. It wasn't long before she saw her brother's signature blond hair, and she slowed down to tag him on the shoulder before running ahead. 'You're it!' she called back over her shoulder. 'Race you to the roos!'

It took a few seconds for Robert to realise what was happening, but then he sprang into action and sprinted after his sister. 'No fair,' Robert yelled, staring at Bindi's bobbing ponytail, 'you had a head start!'

'You snooze, you lose!' teased Bindi, giggling.

The race was on. Despite Bindi having the advantage of a head start, Robert was small and agile – an advantage in a crowded zoo. It was much easier for him to dodge through groups of people and around obstacles that got in the way. They were neck and neck for a while until Bindi got waylaid by a young couple who asked if she could take their picture. Bindi happily obliged and tried to ignore Robert's smirk as he took the lead. After handing back the camera she did her best to catch up to her brother, but to no avail.

'I win!' shouted Robert, triumphantly throwing his hands in the air as he pulled up at the gate to the kangaroo enclosure.

'Well done,' said Bindi, coming a close second.
She pulled out a bottle of water from her backpack
and they shared a drink, still panting from their race.
They made their way through another gate, which
led them into the grassy area where the kangaroos
lived. It was a walk-through enclosure so visitors
could feed and interact with the kangaroos. It was
getting late in the day and most of the visitors had
left, so Bindi and Robert had the macropods all to
themselves.

Bindi loved many things about kangaroos,
but she particularly liked that they were social
creatures, living together in families called mobs.
She scanned the enclosure for a sign of Pebbles.
Pebbles was a red kangaroo – the largest of all the
kangaroos.

'There she is!' Robert pointed to a kangaroo

lying on her side, enjoying the last rays of the day.

Pebbles was a well-known character amongst visitors and keepers alike. She was cheeky and liked to play tricks on the other kangaroos, and was particularly known for creeping up on her roo mates and grabbing their tails with her claws before hopping away. Kangaroos are not able to use their legs independently so they hop using powerful hind legs and their tail for balance. It was very comical to watch Pebbles creating so much mischief while bouncing on two legs!

Bindi and Robert had been overjoyed when Pebbles gave birth to a joey named Tommy. Although small in size, he had plenty of personality. He seemed to have inherited his mother's love of mischief and was a bundle of fun. They slowly approached Pebbles and sat quietly on the grass beside her.

'Hi Pebbles, how's little Tommy going?' asked Robert with a cheeky smile.

The little ball of fluff poked his head out of his mum's pouch and looked about inquisitively. Not one for shyness, Pebbles encouraged Tommy out of her pouch and onto the ground in front of her.

'She wants Tommy to play with us!' gasped Bindi with delight.

Soon Bindi, Robert and Tommy were playing on the grass. Tommy was surprisingly strong and steady on his feet. The zoo keepers had told Bindi he was big for his age and they thought he would grow up to be one of their largest red kangaroos. Bindi and Robert were having so much fun they didn't notice the sun slowly disappearing behind the trees, nor the shadows lengthening across the grass.

The walkie-talkie crackled to life, and Terri's voice alerted them to the lateness of the hour. 'Dinner's nearly ready, team. Over,' Terri called.

'We'll be right there, Mum! Over,' Bindi replied.

As if she had understood every word, Pebbles gathered Tommy up and he hopped back into her pouch.

'Seems like mothers around the zoo are united when it comes to playtime being over!' Robert chuckled, and began to jog in the direction of the gate. 'Last one home's a rotten egg!'

Bindi gave her favourite roo duo a final wave before she turned to give chase.

CHAPTER TWO

OVER THEIR DINNER, BINDI AND
Robert gave their mum an update on Pebbles'
antics.

'She just dumped him on the ground and
nudged him to play with us!' laughed Bindi. 'But

when enough's enough she wrangles him back into her pouch.'

'A pouch could come in handy sometimes,' Terri noted with a wry smile. 'Well, guys, *I* have some news,' continued Terri, between mouthfuls. 'My old friend Amanda Paterson called and she's thinking of visiting with the kids.'

Bindi's ears pricked up at the news. 'That would be fantastic. I miss Damian, and it would be so good to see him again.'

Terri turned to her son. 'You might not remember Katie because you were only little when we last saw them and she was a baby. She's six now.'

Robert smiled and concentrated on spiking as many pieces of green beans onto his fork as possible. His record was ten, but he felt sure it was only a matter of time before he beat it.

Bindi's expression changed as she grew serious. 'How are Amanda and the kids?' she asked.

'She sounded okay on the phone, but she's worried about Damian,' sighed Terri. 'That's why she thought a change of scenery would be a good idea.'

Bindi nodded sadly. Amanda's husband, David, had been killed the previous year while serving with the United States Army in Afghanistan. They lived in Colorado and Terri caught up with her old school friend as often as she could. The news of David's death had come as a big shock to the Irwins.

Terri noticed that Robert was a little quiet and seemed to be attacking his food with more relish than usual. 'You okay, mate?' she asked.

Robert nodded. 'I was just thinking about Dad. I remember he really liked David. They were good mates.'

'You're right, little bro, David and Dad were top mates,' agreed Bindi.

Terri was silent for a moment. It was nearly seven years since Steve had died, and although Terri thought she and the kids were doing a brilliant job of continuing with their lives and Steve's work, she still missed him every single day. She was immensely proud of how Robert and Bindi were managing without their father.

'I think your dad would be really happy to know we can be there for David's family,' Terri smiled encouragingly at the kids. 'Question is, where should we take them on their first visit to Australia?'

Robert perked up immediately. 'That's a no-brainer – Australia Zoo, of course!'

'What about Tasmania?' exclaimed Bindi.

'Or Cape York?' Terri suggested.

'Lady Elliot Island!' added Robert.

'Those are without a doubt our family favourites,' mused Terri. 'All such great and diverse places, it's going to be difficult to choose.'

'How about we go somewhere different?' suggested Bindi.

'A camping trip?' said Robert.

'Or a train trip?' suggested Terri a second later.

They all laughed.

'A camping trip and a train journey sounds tip-top terrific!' giggled Bindi.

'I know!' said Terri, as she jumped up from the table. She left the room while Robert and Bindi continued to come up with other holiday options. Despite the amount of travelling their family did, they never failed to get excited about going somewhere new.

'Here we are,' Terri announced as she sat back down at the table and opened a large hardcover atlas to a map of Australia.

Bindi and Robert leaned in for a better look while Terri's finger traced the outline of Australia as she read out the names of a few places they might visit.

'Sunshine Coast, the western coast . . . or the Top End?' Terri pondered the choices aloud.

'I've got an idea,' Bindi piped up. She placed her finger on the dead centre of the map. 'The Patersons live in rocky mountain country, right? So let's take them on a train trip through the Australian desert and then go camping in the outback. That's about as far from their world as they can get!'

Robert nodded with enthusiasm. 'That's a great idea! We could visit Uluru!'

Though the Irwins had been to Alice Springs a few times, they hadn't visited the area for some years and Amanda's visit would be a great opportunity for them all to see that wonderful part of the world again. There was something both magical and mystical about Uluru and Kata Tjuta, with its red earth and endless blue skies. The area held special memories for Terri, and she thought it was the perfect destination for a family wanting to get away from it all.

Terri leaned back in her chair and, with a decisive nod of the head, said, 'The Red Centre it is!'

CHAPTER THREE

AFTER A FLURRY OF CALLS AND
emails back and forth, the Paterson family booked their flights to Australia. Meanwhile, Bindi, Terri and Robert threw themselves into planning an outback adventure to impress their American visitors.

The trip was to begin in Adelaide, where they would board a train and travel up to Alice Springs. From there they planned to do some sightseeing and hire a four-wheel drive to take them camping near famous geological sites such as Uluru, Kata Tjuta and Watarrka.

The weeks zoomed past until the day dawned which found the Irwin family waiting at the arrivals terminal at Adelaide Airport to meet their American guests. Both Terri and the kids had been extremely busy with their various commitments and were well and truly looking forward to a break.

'I wonder what Damian's into these days?' Bindi asked her mum. 'Do you know if he still plays sport? I remember him being good at just about every sport he played.'

Bindi had great memories of the last time she had seen Damian many years before when they had visited their friends at their home in Denver. At the time, Damian had been right into rock climbing, snowboarding and hiking in the mountains. The two families had gone skiing in nearby Steamboat Springs, and Damian had taught Bindi how to snowboard.

Bindi laughed as she reminisced about the holiday. 'I remember I face-planted right in front of all the cool kids, and Damian just ignored their mocking and helped me up.'

'I'm not too sure of Damian's interests these days,' said Terri, as she brushed her fringe from her eyes and scanned the crowd for her friend. She was dressed in jeans, a blue T-shirt and sturdy walking shoes. She looked ready to take on the outback. 'From what Amanda has told me, he's taken his father's death extremely hard. We'll need to be patient with him.'

Bindi nodded. She understood that everyone dealt with grief in their own way.

'There they are!' Robert pointed to a family of three pushing a trolley of backpacks through the sliding doors. He took off at lightning speed through the crowd to greet them.

'Robert's so fast these days he'll give Damian a run for his money in the sprinting department,' laughed Bindi, as she watched the bundle of blond hair and boyish energy darting through the waiting throng in the arrivals hall.

'You're a sight for sore eyes!' Amanda exclaimed, as she took Robert in her arms. Katie giggled beside them as Robert feigned being unable to breathe from the bear hug he received.

'Hi Robert!' said Katie, as she continued giggling. She was a very pretty girl with dark brown eyes and long dark brown hair that was pulled back into two pigtails. She held a soft-toy giraffe in one hand and twirled one of her pigtails with the other.

'Hi. What's the name of your giraffe?' asked Robert, disentangling himself from Amanda's grasp.

'Hattie,' said Katie, holding it up for Robert to see.

'Pleased to meet you both,' said Robert. He turned his attention to the lanky teen with the same straight dark hair as Katie's. It fell forward in a mop over his dark features. 'Hi Damian,' said Robert cheerily. He was looking forward to having an older boy around.

The lanky teen shifted his weight from one foot to the other, looking distinctly uncomfortable. 'Hey,' he mumbled, avoiding Robert's gaze.

Bindi and Terri approached with huge smiles on their faces.

'Hi Damian!' Bindi could hardly contain her excitement. 'Welcome to Australia!' She went in to give him a big hug but, sensing she needed to hold back, put out a hand instead.

'Hi,' Damian mumbled, and awkwardly shook Bindi's hand before quickly shoving his hand back into his jeans.

'Damian!' Amanda frowned and gave her son a warning look.

Damian scowled back at her and rolled his eyes. He gave Terri a tight smile but made little effort to hide the fact that he didn't want to be there.

Bindi caught her mum's eye. She remembered how mixed up and confused she had felt when she'd lost her dad. She knew it was important to make allowances for Damian's behaviour, no matter how unfriendly he may seem.

'Hi Bindi,' said Katie, shyly. Her giggle rang out again in stark contrast to Damian's surly attitude.

'Great to see you, Katie,' beamed Bindi. 'We've got a pretty exciting week planned for you guys.'

'Yay!' said Katie, flashing the cutest little gap-toothed smile. Bindi thought she was completely adorable.

After a long hug, Terri took Amanda's hands and held them in her own. 'How are you?' she asked.

Amanda took a deep breath and looked her old friend in the eye. 'It's been a rough road, and we're taking it one step at a time.'

Terri nodded. Amanda didn't have to say any more; Terri understood. 'It's so good to see you,' she said with feeling, giving Amanda's hands another squeeze.

Damian sighed and shifted uneasily, as if embarrassed by the emotions on display. He had both hands thrust deep into his pockets and a signature teen slouch. He didn't look at all like the sporty jock Bindi remembered from their last visit.

'It's great to have you guys here,' said Bindi, trying to lighten the mood. 'We're all really excited about the holiday.'

'Good for you,' Damian muttered under his breath, so that his mother couldn't hear. She and Terri had fallen into a conversation about the States as Terri plied Amanda for news about their mutual friends.

Katie seemed oblivious to her brother's bad mood and stood up on the tips of her toes to whisper into Bindi's ear. 'Can we see a kangaroo now?' she asked.

Bindi's eyes widened with delight. A fellow animal lover! 'You might find a fluffy one in the souvenir shop,' she whispered back.

'They don't hop down the street?' asked Katie, her face a picture of disappointment.

'Wait until we get to the outback because that's where you'll get to see the real thing!' reassured Bindi.

Katie smiled her gap-toothed grin again. And Bindi decided that her new mission was to make sure that Katie Paterson was constantly smiling.

CHAPTER FOUR

IT DIDN'T TAKE LONG TO MAKE their way to Adelaide Railway Station, from where their country train would depart. As they pulled into the station they were met with a row of carriages stretching back as far as the eye could see.

'It's enormous!' remarked Amanda, impressed.

'It sure is,' agreed Terri. 'We've been on this trip a few times now and I still get excited by it. There's something about sleeping on a train and listening to the sound of wheels on the track as you drift off to sleep.'

'It sounds deliciously peaceful,' mused Amanda.

They hopped out of the taxi and gazed upon the impressive rows of gleaming silver carriages.

'That is some train,' enthused Robert, as he swung a backpack over his shoulder.

Damian was the only person who failed to look impressed. In fact, he'd spent the entire taxi ride playing his Nintendo 3DS.

'We're here!' Robert said to Damian with a big smile.

'Oh.' Damian glanced up from his game and slunk out of the taxi.

As they made their way down to their platform it struck Bindi that they would be travelling on a historic piece of railway and one of the great train journeys of the world. Once upon a time, the route across the Red Centre was populated by Afghan cameleers who traversed the route. These early pioneers opened up the harsh interior to the rest of Australia. She made a mental note to discuss this in further detail with Sarah when she was back at homeschooling.

As they made their way along the platform, Bindi glanced at the tickets. 'I think we're in B Carriage,' she said as she scanned the letters on the side of the train carriages.

'B for Bindi,' smiled Katie.

'Bindi Irwin?' asked a young porter, who was standing by the carriage door.

'That's me,' smiled Bindi.

'Welcome aboard!' He tipped his hat to the group. 'My name is Darren and I'll be your steward for the next two days. If there's anything you need, you only have to ask.' He motioned to their luggage. 'Your luggage will be taken care of. Hop on and I'll show you to your sleeping quarters.'

'Thank you,' said Terri. 'Nice to meet you, Darren.'

'Woo hoo!' cried Katie, as she bounced up the steps and disappeared inside the train.

Amanda looked momentarily anxious before Terri gave her a reassuring smile. 'Robert and Bindi will keep an eye on her, don't worry.'

Bindi and Robert took the hint and jumped aboard the train to catch up with Katie. Damian loitered on the platform, staring moodily at his feet.

'Do you like trains, Damian?' asked Terri.

He shrugged. 'They're all right, I suppose.'

'You used to love them when you were little,' said Amanda, trying to coax her son to open up.

'I'm not little anymore though, am I, Mum?' asked a surly Damian, bringing the conversation to an abrupt halt once more.

'I'm not little either, but I still think they're fun,' Terri said, and held out her arm for Damian to step onboard before her.

Damian took the hint and disappeared inside.

Terri then held out her hand for Amanda. 'After you, madam,' she said, as she took Amanda's hand to help her onboard.

Amanda gave her friend a grateful smile. 'You have no idea how much I need this holiday,' she whispered.

'You and me both,' Terri replied. The friends linked arms and jostled their way down the corridor in search of their cabins.

They all took a tour of the train's facilities, which included two formal dining carriages, a café, a lounge, a reading room, as well as numerous snack bars and drinks trolleys. The train seemed vast and the kids enjoyed walking the length of the forty carriages.

'Wouldn't it be fun to see how long it would take to run from one end to the other?' suggested Robert.

'Yeah!' agreed Bindi, 'though we'd have to wait until it was empty. Too many potential obstacles otherwise!' She glanced at Damian to see what he thought of the idea. 'Do you still run much?' she asked.

'Nah,' said Damian. He looked uncomfortable at answering the question and turned to stare out of the window. But Bindi was determined not to be put off.

'I remember you used to be very good,' said Bindi. 'You beat me hands down. Remember when –' Bindi was about to launch into a story about the last time they had seen each other, but Damian cut her off.

'Let's find our cabins. I want to lie down.' He turned and walked off in the direction of the sleeping quarters.

'Worst case of jet lag I've ever seen,' Robert remarked to his sister.

Bindi raised an eyebrow but said nothing. 'Come on, let's go check out our rooms!' exclaimed Robert before taking off. They dashed down the corridor to catch up to the others.

The cabins catered to two people. Though compact inside, they made great use of the space available. They came with fold-up bunk beds, a sink and a small table with two chairs.

'Who's going to sleep where?' asked Terri, as she inspected each of the three cabins they had allocated to them.

'Can I share a room with Bindi, *pleeeease*?'

asked Katie, bouncing up and down with excitement.

Terri turned to Amanda. 'It's okay with me if it's okay with Bindi.'

Bindi nodded. 'It's a great idea! It will be like a real girly sleepover. We can stay up talking all night!'

Katie, her mouth agape, looked about ready to squeal when Amanda stopped her. 'Sshh! We have to remember that there are other people on the train. No squealing.' Katie nodded and pretended to zip up her mouth, settling for a big thumbs up in Bindi's general direction.

'If the girls are going to be together then how about Robert and Damian have a boys' sleepover too?' Amanda suggested.

'Um . . . boys don't really do sleepovers like girls,' said Robert hesitantly. He wasn't sure about the idea of being alone in a cabin with the Dark Cloud of Doom that was Damian.

'Do I have to?' Damian scowled. 'He's just a little kid.'

'Damian!' hissed Amanda. Her cheeks flushed with embarrassment at her son's behaviour.

'What?' Damian mouthed back. Mother and son glared at each other.

'It's no biggie,' said Robert quickly. 'I'll share with my mum.' He flashed Damian a big smile. 'She appreciates my company.'

Amanda gave Robert a grateful smile and let out a long exhale, as if mentally schooling herself to be patient.

'How long are we stuck on this train for, anyway?' Damian asked with resignation.

Robert gave him a playful slap on the back. 'Two

whole days. It's a bit like snakes on a plane – there's no escape!'

Damian smiled despite himself. 'That was actually quite funny, little guy.'

Robert puffed up his chest. 'I'm a master of wit,' he said. 'Just one of my many talents.'

The train gave a long toot and, with a shudder the wheels, began to move.

'We're off!' cried Bindi. 'Alice Springs, here we come!'

CHAPTER FIVE

THEY SPENT THE REST OF THE morning enjoying the view from the lounge carriage. As the train was moving at a decent speed, each time Bindi turned to look out of the window the view was of something different. Gone were the outskirts of suburban Adelaide, the suburbs having dissolved into paddocks and clusters of gums.

The majestic Flinders Ranges came into view on the right side of the train. Bindi, Robert and Katie settled comfortably in a booth together while Damian sat by himself on the opposite side of the train. He was busy playing his game again and paid them no attention. The sound of explosions and gunfire emanated from Damian's console, completely at odds with the tranquil atmosphere of the train carriage.

'I spy with my little eye something beginning with C,' Katie said eagerly, clearly enjoying the game.

'Crimson Chat?' asked Bindi.

'What's that?' asked Katie, scrunching up her forehead at the unfamiliar word.

'Bindi's just showing off,' teased Robert. 'It's a bird.'

Katie shook her head. 'Nope.'

'Cockatoo?' said Robert.

Katie shook her head again and giggled.

'Carpet,' said Bindi, pointing to the plush red carpet that ran down the main aisle of the train.

'Nope!'

'Cow?' mumbled Damian, his eyes still glued to his game.

Katie let out a cry of indignation. 'That's not fair, you're not even playing!' She sank back into her seat and folded her arms in a huff.

Damian briefly looked up from his console. 'I don't know how you can call this "I spy wildlife" – all we've seen are cattle and sheep since we've been on this train.'

Katie turned to her brother. 'How would you even know what's outside? All you do is play that stupid game.'

A flash of irritation crossed Damian's face. 'It's not stupid. It requires lots of technical skill, as a matter of fact.'

Bindi was curious. 'What *are* you playing?' she asked.

Damian studied Bindi with suspicion as he weighed up whether to answer her or not. 'It's called *Report for Duty*,' he began hesitantly, as if expecting her to laugh or criticise him.

'What does it do?' Robert asked.

'You fight people with guns and shoot them,' said Katie.

'It's not just about that,' argued Damian. 'There's heaps of strategy and you have to work with a platoon. It's about teamwork and planning as well as being a good shot. And you have to have super-quick reflexes . . .' He stopped abruptly, noticing Katie's look of disapproval, and turned back to his game. 'You wouldn't understand.'

Katie poked out her tongue at her brother.

'It sounds difficult,' said Bindi. She had noticed Damian begin to loosen up once he talked about something he enjoyed, and she wanted to try and keep the conversation going. 'I'm terrible at computer games,' she laughed.

But Damian had turned to stare out of his window and didn't reply.

Katie, unperturbed by her brother's moodiness, pulled at Robert's shirtsleeve. 'Can we keep playing?' she pleaded.

'Sure thing!' smiled Robert. 'Where were we?'

'It's Damian's turn,' pointed out Bindi.

Damian gave a small sigh. 'I spy with my little eye something beginning with . . .' He gave a small smile as he kept the others hanging. 'Nah, I don't want to play. It's a game for babies!' he said, and returned to his game.

Bindi noticed Katie's chin tremble and it looked as if she would cry. She leaned towards Bindi and Robert, and spoke in an exaggerated whisper so that her brother could hear.

'Damian used to be fun to hang out with and then his hormones went crazy and he turned into a teenager.' Katie pulled a face, sat back in her seat then looked out of her window. If Damian had heard what his sister had said he made no sign of it, and continued playing his game.

Bindi and Robert caught each other's gaze.

Befriending Damian was turning out to be more of a challenge than either of them had imagined. Bindi looked out at the view. The farmland had given way to scrub, with occasional eucalypts and a scattering of grazing cattle. Soon she could see more pools of water and more birds. There were large flocks of ducks, groups of crows, and lots of birds of prey.

'Damian has a point about the wildlife,' said Bindi. 'I haven't seen anything other than birds, and we still haven't seen a kangaroo.'

'At home people think kangaroos hop down the street in Australia,' said Katie. 'Where we live there are bears. Sometimes, if you go for a bushwalk, you might run into one.'

'Bonza!' said Robert, impressed. 'Have you seen a bear in the wild?'

51

Katie nodded and her eyes grew wide. 'Once, when I was out snowshoe walking with my dad, we came across a grizzly. There was nothing around except the quiet sound of branches creaking under the weight of the snow, and the crunch of our shoes. All of a sudden my dad just froze. He held out a hand to stop me. At first I didn't realise why, but when I looked up, there was a grizzly directly in front of us.'

'What happened?' asked Bindi, intrigued. She noticed Damian's hands were no longer moving. He had stopped playing and was listening to the story. The sound of guns firing no longer filled the lounge.

'The bear looked at us, and we looked at him. I couldn't have moved even if I'd wanted to. I was petrified,' said Katie.

'I'm sure you were. I've seen a few grizzlies in my time and they are humungous!' said Bindi. 'So what did you do?'

Katie's eyes grew large as she recounted the memory. 'My dad remained so calm and clear-headed. He was very brave, although he told me later that he was also frightened. He pulled me behind him and we walked backwards in the snow until the bear was out of sight. Then we turned and hightailed it back home as fast as we could.' Katie gave a laugh.

'That's a great story,' said Bindi. 'Your dad did the right thing.'

'We did lots more walks, but we never saw a bear again.' Katie glanced over at Damian before continuing. 'I miss those walks.'

They sat in companionable silence until they heard the sound of a scream and an explosion. Damian had recommenced playing his game.

The constant noise of ammunition firing was beginning to grate.

'Damian, can you please put on some head-phones or mute the sound? It's giving me a headache,' requested Amanda from a booth further down the carriage where she was sitting with Terri.

Damian rolled his eyes and slumped further down into the couch. He muttered to himself as he pulled out a headset and plugged it into the console. The explosions and gunfire ceased, and the sounds in the carriage reverted to a low murmur of conversation and the odd clink of cutlery on a plate.

'Finally, some peace and tranquility,' smiled Amanda, as she took a sip of her mineral water. 'Even my knots have knots,' she grimaced as she rubbed at her neck.

'So how is it going, *really*?' Terri asked her friend.

Amanda let out a long sigh before speaking. 'Katie's going to be fine. She misses David but she hasn't gone off the rails or anything. It's Damian I'm worried about.'

Terri nodded. 'He's certainly hurting,' she agreed.

'I tried to get him to see a grief counsellor but he refused. He won't open up to me and, as far as I know, he hasn't really talked to any of his friends,' said Amanda. 'Thing is, I don't know where the line between teen angst begins and grief ends.

It's all blurry so I try to cut him lots of slack, but I also think he takes advantage of that.'

Terri gave her friend a consoling look. 'He'll get there in time.'

Amanda nodded. 'I know you can't rush the grieving process, but what really worries me is his obsession with this computer game,' she said, gesturing in Damian's direction. 'It's a war game that involves fighting strategy – it's like he's obsessing over the way David died by playing the game. It can't be healthy.'

'Just wait until we get him to the outback,' said Terri. 'A bit of open air and a taste of the natural environment will bring him back to earth.'

'I hope so,' said Amanda wearily. She gave Terri a sad smile before looking back at her son.

CHAPTER SIX

AFTER PORT AUGUSTA THEY
were treated to a stunning sunset over the red
earth. Under the blanket of darkness, landscape
became sandscape until it was impossible to
see anything in the dark that lay beyond their
windows.

It was dinnertime and, despite having spent most of the day sitting on the train, they were all famished. The tables in the formal dining carriage had been beautifully set with red tablecloths and a small candle, and the room was ambient with dimmed lighting.

'Good evening,' said Darren, as he made his way around their table, handing out menus and placing a napkin onto each of their laps.

They all murmured their greetings as they avidly studied the menu.

'I'll give you some time to look over the menu. But first, I'll let you know about our special this evening.' Darren expertly poured water into their glasses as he spoke. 'Our special tonight is a kangaroo fillet in a wild mushroom sauce with a side of vegetables. I thoroughly recommend it.'

Amanda turned pale. 'Did you just say what I think you said?' she asked.

Darren looked at her blankly. 'I'm sorry?'

'Did you mean kangaroo, as in hop hop?' asked Katie, her face ashen.

Darren smiled hesitantly. 'Is there a problem?' he asked, obviously confused.

Terri held up her hand. 'Thanks, Darren, it's okay. We'll have a look at the menus and order in a few minutes.'

Darren continued to pour the water while they looked over their menus in silence. When he had moved away to another table, Amanda couldn't contain herself any longer. 'What's with kangaroo being on the menu? Isn't it a national icon?' she asked, clearly aghast.

Terri placed her menu on the table. 'There is

a market here that promotes kangaroo as bush meat,' she explained.

'Ew!' exclaimed Katie, as she screwed up her face.

'On the one hand, there's all this propaganda pushing people to believe kangaroos are a pest and in plague proportions and have to be culled to avoid destroying Australia's environment. On the other hand, they are told to believe we should only eat kangaroo as they are good for our environment, unlike livestock. It's a very strange argument,' explained Terri.

'I thought everyone loved kangaroos?' said Amanda. 'Do Australians eat koalas too?' she added, hesitantly.

'No!' said Bindi, shaking her head in horror at the suggestion.

'To make it worse, past regulations haven't been strict enough about quality control. Samples of kangaroo fillets, kebabs, and mince that have been tested have shown traces of E. coli and salmonella,' Terri continued.

'I don't think anyone at this table will be having the special,' Amanda said with a grimace.

Damian shrugged. 'What's the big deal? They're just an animal like any other. Why should they get special treatment?'

'Because killing native wildlife always leads to the endangerment or extinction of that species,' explained Bindi. 'Look what happened with passenger pigeons in America – they were shot to extinction. Tigers are killed for traditional medicine and are critically endangered. We're even battling to protect gorillas from the bush meat trade!'

'Bindi's right,' said Terri. 'In some areas of Australia some kangaroos are scarce and some macropods are critically endangered.'

'What's a macropod?' asked Katie.

'It means the marsupial family. It includes kangaroos, wallabies, bettongs and others,' explained Bindi.

'This is all a bit shocking,' said Amanda, as she placed her menu face down on the table and took a sip of water.

'I'm not saying everyone should become vegetarian,' said Terri. 'We should support our graziers by eating beef, pork, lamb and chicken. Eating bush meat doesn't support the men and women on the land. We cannot expect the entire world to become vegetarian, but we could get the world to stop consuming our native wildlife!'

Terri was interrupted as Darren appeared at the table with a notepad and pen in hand. 'Are you ready to order?' he asked.

'How about a round of toasted sandwiches?' suggested Terri with a bright smile.

Later that night Bindi and Katie were happily tucked into their beds, with Katie on the top bunk and Bindi below. The sound of the train moving along the tracks was quite hypnotic and the gentle swaying motion of the carriages was lulling Bindi to sleep.

'It must be awesome to live in a zoo,' said Katie, as she leant over and gazed down at Bindi.

Bindi opened her eyes. 'It sure is! You'll have to come visit us sometime.'

'I'd like that,' said the cheeky upside-down face.

'Is it strange to be away from home?' asked Bindi.

Katie scrunched up her face. 'Kind of, but then home hasn't felt like home since Dad died.' Katie's face disappeared from view as she lay back in her bed.

'Do you miss *your* dad?' asked Katie in a quiet voice.

'Every single day,' Bindi whispered.

'Me too,' replied Katie.

'You know,' mused Bindi, 'if I'm missing him lots and it's hurting more than usual, I try to think of stories about him that make me happy. Like your bear story.'

'Can you tell me one?' asked Katie.

Bindi looked up at the wooden bed frame above

her. In an instant she was back in time sitting next to her dad on an aeroplane. 'I remember one time when I was only three years old,' began Bindi. 'We were on a four-week trip around the States to promote a movie. We spent so much time in airports and on the plane that Dad taught me to write my name. I can still picture the look on his face – his smiling eyes – when I proudly showed him that I had written my name for the first time.'

'That's a nice story,' said Katie sleepily. 'Thanks for sharing it with me.'

They both lay in their beds listening to the sounds of the train.

'Dad and I used to make pancakes together,' whispered Katie. 'It was our thing. We would make the batter together. I would pour the mixture into the pan and Dad would toss them perfectly. Then we'd call Mum and Damian and we'd all stuff ourselves silly. I used to look forward to it every time he came home from leave.'

'I can just picture you all together doing that!' laughed Bindi. 'It sounds like fun.'

'It was,' said Katie, smiling at the memory

Bindi could feel her eyelids grow heavier. She rolled onto her side and mumbled, 'Night, Katie.'

'Night, Bindi,' whispered Katie, and closed her eyes.

CHAPTER SEVEN

LYING IN HER BED, BINDI COULD see through a crack in the curtains that they had entered the desert overnight and were now deep into it. It was all red earth and saltbush as far as she could see. Although it looked as if they were in the Northern Territory, Bindi knew that this was still South Australia. This train trip was an immediate reminder that Australia was a vast country.

The sky had turned to fiery ripples of red as dawn exploded on the landscape, while orange and pink rays stretched across the wide expanse of earth. Bindi rubbed her eyes and sat up. Today they would disembark from the train in Alice Springs, and the next phase of their adventure would begin.

She hopped out of bed and stepped onto the bottom rung of the ladder to peer up to the bunk above to see if Katie was still asleep.

'Morning!' said a very awake-looking Katie, who was also enjoying the view through the curtain.

Bindi grinned. 'What do you say to some breakfast?'

'I'm starved!' Katie threw off the sheets and clambered down the ladder to join Bindi. The girls giggled as they kept knocking into one another, trying to maintain their balance while getting dressed.

Soon Bindi and Katie met up with Robert, Terri and Amanda in the café, which opened early to cater for those who enjoy the sunrise with something in their stomach.

'Where's Damian?' asked Katie, looking around.

'He wanted to sleep in,' Amanda replied. 'I don't think wild horses could have dragged him down from that top bunk so I left him to it.'

'More food for us then!' exclaimed Robert, before making his way over to the buffet table.

The gang chatted as they enjoyed a leisurely breakfast of fresh pastries, fruit, eggs and toast.

'Alice Springs is a funny name,' mused Katie, as she munched on her vegemite toast.

'Early settlers thought that there was a permanent waterhole in the Todd River and they named it after the wife of the former postmaster general, Sir Charles Todd. Little did they know that the river is usually dry,' explained Bindi.

'Did you know that Alice Springs is in the geographic centre of Australia?' asked Robert, as he tucked into his third serving of a generous-sized croissant with jam.

'We're going to the Red Centre in the dead centre!' sang Katie.

'It's such an amazing place, I can't wait for you to see it!' said Bindi.

'Oh,' Robert groaned suddenly, clutching his stomach.

'What's wrong?' asked Amanda, alarmed that Robert had fallen ill.

'I'm beginning to think my third helping was a mistake,' Robert moaned, and rubbed his swollen belly.

'Not to worry!' laughed Terri. 'It will be simple camp food for the next few days so enjoy it while you can.'

Late morning saw the train cross the Finke River. The dry channel was claimed as one of the world's most ancient rivers. It was normally no more than a series of waterholes along a wide and dusty bed, but when flooded, it flowed hundreds of kilometres to Lake Eyre. A couple of hours later they were through Heavitree Gap, and the train slowed as it pulled into Alice Springs.

Once their bags were safely stowed at their bed and breakfast, it was time to get organised by buying the supplies for their outback expedition.

'All right, gang, I need to hire the four-wheel drive, get camping supplies, food and a satellite phone,' said Terri, as they all gathered in the main street.

'What can we do to help?' asked Amanda.

'I'd rather you all took in some sights. There's so much to do in Alice that I'd hate for you to miss anything, and I'll probably get it done more quickly on my own,' smiled Terri.

'Awesome!' exclaimed Robert. 'You know where we're going first, don't you?' he asked with a big grin.

'Where?' asked Damian, warily.

'You'll see,' said Robert. 'Remember what I said about snakes on a plane?'

CHAPTER EIGHT

THE ALICE SPRINGS REPTILE Centre showcased the largest collection of reptiles in Central Australia, and Robert had already made sure to memorise every reptile they held. Robert had been very young the last time he had visited so he was extra excited to be able to visit the centre now that he was eight years old and equipped with a fairly hefty knowledge of reptiles.

As they entered the centre, he was quick to point out a few of the attractions.

'There's a saltwater crocodile, a huge perentie goanna, frill-necked lizards and thorny devils!' Robert began in an excited ramble. 'Not to mention large and small pythons and some of the world's most venomous snakes, such as fierce snakes, brown snakes, death adders and king brown snakes!'

'Why are we here again?' asked Katie, who was beginning to look decidedly nervous at the thought of so many reptiles under the same roof.

Bindi held her hand. 'Don't worry, we'll have you handling a snake in no time!' she teased.

'This is actually pretty cool,' enthused Damian,

as he watched an olive python unwrapping itself from around a thick branch.

'Told you!' said Robert, before dashing off to check out another display.

After wandering around on their own for a while, they were introduced to one of the tour guides, Sam, a reptile enthusiast who was only too keen to sound off with Robert about all things reptilian.

'Who would like to handle Doug?' asked Sam.

'Damian!' Robert volunteered with a cheeky grin.

Damian shrugged. 'Sure.' Then a thought occurred to him. 'Who's Doug?'

'He's our beautiful olive python,' said Sam. He leant into the enclosure and picked up the snake Damian had been admiring earlier.

Damian baulked but, not wanting to lose face in front of everyone, least of all Robert, remained silent.

Sam smiled reassuringly. 'Don't worry, olive pythons have a very gentle nature and are perfect snakes to handle,' he explained, while Doug began to slowly travel up Damian's arm.

'How do pythons eat their prey?' asked Robert, a picture of innocence.

'Good question, Robert,' said Sam, before launching into an enthusiastic explanation. 'They constrict their prey by coiling themselves around the animal or bird. They can even eat small animals up to the size of a bandicoot or a young wallaby.'

'Is that so?' asked Robert, fascinated.

'Yep! And they don't crush their prey but rather severely restrict movement,' continued Sam. 'As the prey breathes out, the tightening coils prevent the prey from inhaling. So the snake's prey very quickly suffocates. To accomplish this, pythons are extremely muscular and usually heavy-bodied snakes.'

Meanwhile, Doug had wound his way up Damian's arm and behind his head so that he was now wrapped around Damian's neck.

'Does he feel like a muscular and heavy-bodied snake, Damian?' asked Robert.

Damian narrowed his eyes and glared at Robert, before turning to Sam. 'Is this a good idea?'

'He's fine,' chuckled Sam. 'He's just being affectionate.'

'Don't move, sweetheart, while I take a photo,' said Amanda, as she pulled a digital camera from her handbag.

'I'm not about to move a muscle, Mum,' answered Damian dryly.

Robert stepped beside Damian and put his arm around him, and they both smiled for the camera.

'Cheese!' said Amanda, as she took the picture. She checked the photo she had just taken. 'Oh, that's a great one of you boys,' she gushed.

Robert held out an arm and encouraged Doug to come to him. 'Here, matey,' he crooned, 'come to Robert.'

With expert ease Robert was able to relieve Damian of Doug and look completely at home holding the five-metre snake.

'You're a natural, Robert,' praised Sam.

With grudging respect, Damian watched Robert relate to the snake with no trace of anxiety. The little guy was completely at home holding a mature python which probably weighed twice as much as Robert.

'I held my first snake before I was even two years old,' said Robert. 'My dad helped me. I was too little to hold a big snake on my own so Dad and I would sit on the ground and let the python slither all over us. That's probably the earliest memory I have of holding a snake.'

'Your dad did a fine job,' said Sam.

Robert held Doug out to Damian. 'Want to try again?' he asked.

Damian nodded. 'I'll try again,' he said, and held out his arms to take the snake.

CHAPTER NINE

THE NEXT MORNING IT WAS TIME
to leave Alice Springs and hit the road. Eager to
make an early start, the gang greeted another
spectacular sunrise as they piled into a hired four-
wheel drive.

Once everyone was buckled in, Terri started

the engine and made her way out of town and onto the main highway.

Damian rubbed his bleary eyes. 'I don't see why we had to get up so early,' he moaned.

'So we can have more time to do stuff, silly,' giggled Katie, as if it was obvious.

'Yeah right, silly me,' muttered Damian. He unzipped his backpack and searched through its contents.

'I didn't realise Uluru wasn't actually in Alice,' confessed Amanda.

'It takes nearly five hours to get there,' noted Terri, 'but we'll be there with plenty of time for lunch and then we can spend the afternoon exploring.'

'Has anyone seen my console?' asked Damian, grumpily.

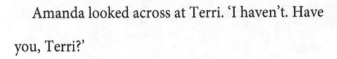

Amanda looked across at Terri. 'I haven't. Have you, Terri?'

Terri shook her head. 'Sorry, Damian. Are you sure you didn't leave it with the other gear we stored at the bed and breakfast?'

Damian shook his head adamantly. 'No, I know I packed it!' He went through his backpack one more time, this time pulling out all of its contents onto the seat beside him.

Then it dawned on him. He met his mother's eyes through the rear-view mirror. 'Stealing is an offence, you know.'

'Technically, I didn't steal it as I paid for it in the first place,' Amanda said, smiling sweetly at her son. After a pause, she turned around to face Damian. 'I'm sorry, I had to make an executive decision. It was my sanity versus your need to play a game. And my sanity won!'

'Ugh!' huffed Damian in exasperation. He turned to stare out the window. Bindi and Robert shared a look. Damian was proving to be one tough customer!

There wasn't much to see on the highway as they left Alice Springs. Damian had expected to see the countryside filled with wildlife, but all he saw was barren land – and lots of it. He noted a road sign that featured a hopping kangaroo. Maybe they'd get to see some wildlife after all.

They had only been on the highway for less than ten minutes when Terri slowed down.

'What's up?' asked Robert.

'There's a kangaroo on the side of the road,' said Bindi.

'Where?' exclaimed Katie, straining her neck to see.

'I don't see . . .' Damian trailed off as he realised the kangaroo was not hopping past them but lying by the side of the road.

'Is it alive?' asked Katie.

'Sorry, honey,' said Terri, as she pulled over. 'It looks like she's been hit by a car.'

'How do you know it's a female?' asked Damian.

'Females are smaller than males,' explained Terri, 'and I can see she has a pouch.'

'She's not breathing, Mum,' said Bindi, studying the kangaroo intently. Terri nodded sadly and checked her rear-view mirror. She waited for a truck to come hurtling past before she pulled out onto the highway.

Bindi took one last look at the doe, then cried, 'Wait, Mum! Stop the car!' She unbuckled her seatbelt hastily.

'What is it, Bindi?' asked Terri, as she once again pulled the car over to the side of the road.

'I think I saw something moving!' exclaimed Bindi, before leaping out of the four-wheel drive.

Bindi approached the lifeless kangaroo with care and knelt down next to its large body. She ran her hand over its short reddish coat and slowly moved her hand down towards the kangaroo's belly where the pouch was located. As she did this, she noticed a bulging movement coming from the pouch. There was something inside!

'She's got a joey in her pouch!' cried Bindi. The others crowded around and peered down at the kangaroo.

'What's a pouch?' asked Katie.

'It's a pocket where the baby kangaroo, called a joey, completes its postnatal development,' explained Terri. 'Joeys are the size of cherries when first born, but they continue to grow and feed from inside the mother's pouch.'

Robert handed Bindi a blanket he had fetched from the car. All eyes were fixed on the kangaroo's belly. Bindi carefully placed her hand inside the pouch and felt around for the joey. 'He's furred,' she told her mum, sounding relieved. This was good news because if the joey was very young or only just furred then its lips would be fused permanently to its mother's teat, and it would be harmful for Bindi to try to remove it from the pouch.

'Go ahead,' encouraged Terri. She felt confident in Bindi's experience from working at the Australia

Zoo Wildlife Hospital that Bindi knew what she was doing.

Bindi wrapped her hand in the blanket and reached inside the pouch again. This allowed the mother's scent to be transferred to the blanket. She carefully pulled out the little joey. He was barely bigger than her hand, and no more than a few months old. He flinched at being outside the warm pouch and curled up into a ball.

'Cute!' cried Katie, as she clutched Amanda's leg.

'Is it okay?' asked Amanda, softly.

Bindi placed the joey on the blanket and carefully wrapped it up. 'Its breathing is a little shallow. I think it's dehydrated.'

'Quickly wrap him in the blanket,' instructed Terri. 'He's suffering from shock. We need to keep him pouched so that he feels safe.'

Bindi carefully wrapped the joey up in the blanket and held him in her arms.

'He's tiny,' breathed Amanda. 'How long do you think he's been on his own?'

'Hard to say,' said Terri, 'but I agree with Bindi – he looks both dehydrated and malnourished. We need to get him some mother's milk – and fast!'

'We've got some milk in the car,' suggested Amanda.

Terri shook her head. 'Cow's milk is dangerous to joeys as they are lactose intolerant. It could even kill him.'

'Then what do we do?' asked Damian.

'There's a kangaroo sanctuary on the other side of Alice Springs,' said Terri. 'I know the owners. They're sure to have some joey formula.'

Bindi held onto her precious parcel and carefully climbed back into the car. 'Don't worry,' she whispered to the joey, 'we'll get you some help.'

Terri turned the car around and headed back towards Alice Springs.

CHAPTER TEN

IT TOOK JUST OVER TWENTY minutes for them to backtrack and find their way to the kangaroo sanctuary run by Jenny and Len Symington. Terri had met them on previous visits to Alice Springs with Steve and had been greatly impressed with their ongoing dedication to nurturing injured roos and orphaned joeys.

'Originally, Jenny and Len used to take in orphans and look after them in their home. Word spread about their's being the place to go to if you found a joey whose parents had been killed by a vehicle,' Terri explained, as they exited the car and approached the main gate to the centre. 'They soon had to build a housing area as they couldn't move for all the kangaroos! The centre has expanded at a huge rate over the last ten years. It's now a big tourist attraction and is run with the help of volunteers and donations from the public.'

They made their way through the main gate and approached the reception area. A teenage girl gave them a wave in greeting. She was wearing a homemade cotton pouch, just like a sling that a new mother would wear with a baby, only the head peeking out belonged to a joey!

'Hi, I'm Cath,' she smiled, 'and this is Tiger.' She pointed to the cute and mischievous-looking joey, who was busy sizing up the new visitors. 'Can I help you?'

'We just found a little joey by the side of the road whose mum was hit by a car. He needs urgent attention. Are Len or Jenny around?' asked Terri.

Cath glanced at a clock that hung on the wall of the office behind her. 'If you're quick you might just catch them, they're heading off into the desert.'

The group followed Cath and Tiger as they wound their way past various enclosures that housed joeys of different sizes. They reached a cute brick cottage with a wide wraparound verandah, and made their way to the back. They found a grey-haired and bearded man in a checked shirt loading equipment onto a dusty red ute. He looked up as the group approached.

'Len!' cried Terri.

'Terri Irwin!' he exclaimed in surprise. 'And friends,' he added as he took in Terri's entourage. He held out a rough hand to shake hers. 'To what do I owe the pleasure?'

'Just loading you up with another patient, Len,' laughed Terri, and pointed to the bundle in Bindi's arms.

'You've travelled a long way,' said Len quizzically.

'We're on holiday,' Terri explained. 'We found him less than an hour ago but I'd say he's been on his own for at least one night, if not more.'

'Come inside,' said Len. 'Let's have a look at

him.' Len made his way up the front steps and inside the house. 'Jenny! Incoming!' he called. Then he turned to them and gestured vaguely to a large oak table. 'Sit, sit!' He opened the fridge and pulled out a feeding bottle. 'Now, first things first. Let's get this fella some grub, then we can make proper introductions,' he said, as he grabbed a saucepan and proceeded to warm up the formula.

The group all found somewhere to sit just as a tall grey-haired woman walked into the room. She was lanky in build with wiry arms and legs, her skin was tanned and she wore loose cotton pants, a T-shirt and thongs.

'Ah, Jen,' announced Len, looking up from the saucepan, 'we have company.'

Jenny recognised Terri and let out a cry of pleasure. 'So good to see you,' she said, and turned to look at the kids in amazement. 'I don't believe it – look how much Bindi and Robert have grown.'

'They're fourteen and eight now,' said Terri proudly.

'How time flies,' exclaimed Len. He poured the warmed formula back into the bottle and tested the temperature on his wrist. 'Good to go. Let's take a look at him.'

Len pulled up a chair next to Bindi, sat down and gently unwrapped the blanket. He peered at the joey, then picked up the bottle and proceeded to give him a feed. The joey didn't struggle at all and, after a few attempts, managed to latch onto the teat and begin sucking noisily.

'You found him just in time,' said Len. 'He needs plenty of fluids, quiet and warmth. If he gets those he might just be all right. And he's a he, in case you were wondering.'

'I was,' said Bindi with a grin.

'Here, you take him,' Len handed the feeding joey back to Bindi. 'He'll need 24-hour care just like any new baby. No handling between feeds. He needs to sleep as much as possible inside his pouch because the rest time in the pouch is critical to a joey's growth and development.'

'You might have noticed that our volunteers wear their joeys in slings as we try to imitate their natural mother as much as possible through the warmth of our body and our heartbeat,' added Jenny, as she gave the bundle a once-over.

'Bindi has looked after many of our patients at the wildlife hospital,' remarked Terri. 'She's a good nurse.'

'I'm sure she is,' said Jenny, giving Bindi a wink. 'Tea, anyone?'

After a couple of enthusiastic nods from Terri and Amanda, Jenny busied herself with preparing the tea and refreshments.

Len turned to face Katie. 'Now, who do we have here?' He leaned forward as if to shake Katie's hand but instead reached his hand up to her ear and produced a one-dollar coin. 'How did that get there?' he laughed. 'Are you in the habit of keeping coins in your ear, young lady?'

Katie giggled and shook her head.

Len placed the coin in her hand. 'Take a good look at it.'

Katie turned the gold coin over in her hands. 'It's got kangaroos on it!' she exclaimed.

'That's right. The kangaroo is a national symbol

of Australia. It's on the Australian coat of arms and on some of our currency. And yet people from overseas, like you, seem to hold the kangaroo in a higher regard than some Australians do,' said Len.

'You even eat them!' exclaimed Katie, remembering the incident on the train.

Len nodded. 'That's right. There's a small market out there for kangaroo meat, although I prefer chicken or fish myself.'

'I'd forgotten you were a magician,' chuckled Terri.

'Amateur magician,' said Len, and glanced meaningfully at Robert and Damian. 'So you boys better be on your toes or I could turn you both into galahs!'

'What's a galah?' Damian whispered to Robert.

'An Australian bird,' Robert whispered back,

'or a silly person. I'm not sure which one he means.'

Jenny placed a pot of bush tea and a jug of lemonade on the table. 'Help yourselves,' she said, handing around a plate of Anzac biscuits.

'Well, it's lovely to see you all, but I'm afraid I have a date with the outback,' said Len, as he stood up and brushed biscuit crumbs from his pants.

'Good to see you, Len,' said Terri. 'We don't want to keep you from your work.'

'It gets lonely out there, you know,' Len said with a glint in his eye. With a flourish he produced a bouquet of pale blue plastic carnations and handed it to Bindi.

'Wow!' she exclaimed.

Quick as a flash his hand brushed Damian's ear

and produced a five-dollar note, which Len handed to Damian.

Damian inspected it. 'Can I keep it?' he asked Len with the hint of a smile.

'Sure,' said Len, as he assessed the teenager. 'If you're looking for some excitement, how about you and Bindi keep me company in the outback?' he said, stroking his beard thoughtfully.

CHAPTER ELEVEN

'YOU CAN'T SEND ME OFF INTO the desert with *him*,' Damian hissed to his mother in exasperation. 'The guy is completely bonkers!'

'"Eccentric" is the term I'd use,' said Amanda, as she took Damian's backpack out of their four-wheel drive. 'If Terri trusts him then I do too.'

She handed the pack to Damian with a look that meant the matter was settled.

Damian shook his head. 'I can't believe you're doing this.'

'I think some time with an adult male will be good for you,' his mother said softly, putting an arm around her son.

'Do you mean Len or the kangaroo?' growled Damian.

They watched as Len finished securing Houdini, a large red buck, into the wire enclosure he had on the back of his ute. The kangaroo stared out at them from behind the wire fence, his ears twitching expectantly.

'Is he a magician too?' asked Katie.

'No, but he's an escape artist, the like of which I had never seen before,' explained Len. 'He was forever escaping as a joey. I can't remember the amount of times I had to go and find the little devil. He had no idea he wouldn't survive without my formula. But now he's a young adult, it's time for him to leave home.'

Katie hopped up and down on the spot. 'Can I go too, please?'

Amanda shook her head. 'I'm sorry, monkey, but this trip is strictly for the older kids.'

'I was hoping you and Robert would stay here with me,' Jenny said to Katie with a wink. 'I have so many joeys who need looking after, and I bet you'd be fantastic as a joey mother.'

Katie's eyes shone with delight. 'I can stay with the kangaroos?' she asked, hopefully.

Jenny nodded. 'It's hard work though, mind. You'll be run off your feet.'

Katie nodded with enthusiasm, not allowing anyone to deter her from being a kangaroo mother.

'If you're sure you can fit us all in?' asked Terri.

Jenny laughed. 'I think at maximum capacity we once housed fifteen joeys in this house before the expansion so I think we can squeeze in four humans. It'll be a treat to have some young people around.'

Robert nodded earnestly. 'You say that now . . .'

Everyone laughed.

Len clapped his hands together. 'Let's get your joey ready for travel, Bindi. You'll need a sling and enough formula for three days. Does he have a name yet?'

Bindi shook her head. 'I'm having trouble thinking of a name. Damian, do you have any ideas?'

Damian shifted uncomfortably and shrugged. 'I don't know . . . Frank?' He blushed with embarrassment.

'Frank?' queried Robert, as he looked at the little joey.

'Frank's a perfect name!' exclaimed Len. 'Bindi might be his new mother but she's going to need your help, Damian. Congratulations, you are now a joey father.'

With that he gave Jenny a quick peck on the cheek, nodded to the others and hopped into the ute behind the wheel. Damian turned once more to Amanda with a pleading expression on his face. She kissed him on the cheek and whispered, 'Have fun!'

Damian grunted in reply and reluctantly climbed into the ute.

'We will!' cried Bindi. She waved goodbye, her sling firmly attached to her shoulders with Frank fitted snugly inside.

'Len, what did you mean when you said that some Australians don't respect the kangaroo?' asked Bindi.

Bindi was seated in the middle with Damian on the passenger side and Len behind the wheel of the ute. Houdini was lying down on a rug in the back of the cab, safe inside his enclosure.

Len cocked his head. 'At least six species of macropods have become extinct since Europeans arrived in Australia. Several more are endangered. In some areas of Australia – though not every area,

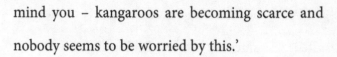

mind you – kangaroos are becoming scarce and nobody seems to be worried by this.'

'Why do you love them so much?' Damian asked.

Len flicked the indicator and turned right onto the main highway that would lead them to Uluru.

'While Jenny and I couldn't have kids, we both felt like we had a lot to give. It happened by accident, really. One day we found a joey whose mother had been killed by a hunter. Now, in kangaroo culls, joeys are often orphaned and left to starve to death while their parents can often die a slow and gruesome death. We'd never seen it firsthand before. After Jenny and I saw the remains of a kill, we were never the same people again. Saving kangaroos became our life.'

'Well, the centre looks amazing – it's twice the size it was since we last saw it!' Bindi gushed.

'Word spread and we have joeys brought in from all over now,' continued Len. 'We open to the public as a way of educating people about what we do but also because seeing a kangaroo is a world-class tourist attraction, and it's getting harder for tourists to see them in the wild. What these idiots who support hunting don't realise is that the kangaroo is worth more to the rural and tourist economy alive than dead.'

Bindi smiled. Listening to Len talk was like listening to her father talk about Australia Zoo and his mission to save endangered species all over the world. There was an emotion in his voice when he spoke, a passion which gave him the energy to keep doing something he believed in no matter how hard it became.

'So how do you do the trick with the note?' Damian asked.

'Aha!' chortled Len. 'A magician, even an amateur one, never reveals his secrets.' He smiled to himself as he continued driving.

CHAPTER TWELVE

LONG BEFORE THEY REACHED
their destination, they could see the huge
sandstone outcrop that was Uluru, rising
up steeply from the desert floor. It had an oasis-
like quality, appearing closer than it actually
was.

'That's some rock,' said Damian, impressed. 'I've seen it in pictures but they're nothing compared to the real thing.'

'It's not one of the seven natural wonders of the world for nothing!' said Len proudly.

The rock was a stunning array of colours in red, brown and grey, which frequently changed as they grew closer. Huge rivets traversed the rock, making its shape look much less like the neat dome that appeared in travel brochures and far more interesting to look at.

'Now, some Uluru stats for our guests,' announced Len. 'It rises 348 metres above the desert and has a circumference of 9.4 kilometres. It's 3.6 kilometres long and 2.4 kilometres wide.'

'It's also full of springs and waterholes, rock

caves and aboriginal paintings,' added Bindi. 'It's a special, sacred place.'

'It's incredible,' said Damian, as he gazed out the window.

'What's even more incredible is that, like an iceberg, there is more of Uluru *under* the ground than above it. Try to get your head around that!' Len exclaimed. 'I've gazed upon Uluru more times than I can remember and I still get chills when I look at it.'

'How is it even possible in the middle of all this . . . flatness?' asked Damian.

'Get ready for the geography lesson,' chuckled Len. 'Bindi, perhaps you can begin?'

Bindi nodded. 'Uluru is an inselberg, which means "island mountain". It's the only remnant left after the slow erosion of the original ancient mountain range.'

Damian nodded in understanding. 'Why did it survive and the rest of the mountain didn't?'

'I'll answer that,' said Len. 'It's because there's a lack of jointing or parting at bedding surfaces, which means that there's no build up of scree or soil which, in turn, means there is no erosion. That's why it survived.'

Len turned off the main highway and headed down a dirt road. They bumped their way along for ten minutes until Len pulled into a private driveway.

'Here we are,' Len announced, as he brought the ute to a halt. 'Some mates of mine live here and won't mind us camping on their land.'

Len hopped out and held the door open for Bindi to clamber down. Frank was fast asleep, strapped inside his homemade pouch and listening to Bindi's heartbeat. Damian got out on the passenger's side and spied two men approaching. They had dark skin and looked like they were of Aboriginal descent.

'Len, you old codger,' one of the men cried with a broad grin.

'Mike!' called Len, and shook the man's hands. 'G'day, Oz,' he said, as he clapped the other man on the back. 'I'd like you guys to meet Bindi and Damian.'

'Nice to meet you,' said Mike, the taller of the two.

'Hi,' said Bindi, flashing them a smile. Damian nodded to the two men and shook their hands.

'These two brothers give tours around the base of the rock and know as much about this part of the world as it is possible to know,' said Len proudly. 'They're of the Pitjantjatjara tribe, one of two Aboriginal tribes who are Anangu – custodians of Uluru.'

'It keeps changing colour,' said Damian, pointing to Uluru.

Mike looked around and lowered his voice. 'Not many people know this, but the rock changes colour because it's inhabited by a wicked Aboriginal spirit. When the spirit is angry it glows red and when the spirit is happy, because of the rainfall, the rock's colour changes to pale grey.' He nodded meaningfully at Damian.

'Really?' asked Damian, his eyes wide.

Mike laughed. 'Nah, just messing with you. Uluru is made of feldspar-rich sandstone called arkose, which is mainly grey and white. The rust colour is caused by a thin coating of iron oxide on the outer skin. The changing colours of red at sunset are caused by light refraction as the sun sinks in the sky. The lower the sun goes, the more it has to travel through the earth's atmosphere, which bends the blue light away, leaving the red light to intensify the rock's red colour.'

'I see,' said Damian flatly.

'Now that that's settled, let's rustle up some grub,' said Len. 'I'm starved.'

'I'll get a fire going,' volunteered Oz.

While the men set about their duties, Bindi turned to Damian. 'Would you like to nurse Frank?'

'Nah,' said Damian, backing away from the group. 'I'll just have a look round.'

'Excellent idea,' called Len. 'We'll get some

lunch together. Check out the dunny – it's an experience you'll never forget.'

Damian rolled his eyes at Len's relentless good humour and turned away.

Mike raised an eyebrow. 'Not a very happy camper, is he?' he noted.

'I'm sure he's got his reasons,' said Len. 'Let's get Houdini settled and see about some food.'

As Bindi watched Damian's retreating figure, she absently stroked Frank's furry little head. 'I'm going to need your help to win him over, Frank,' she said. 'That boy needs a friend.'

CHAPTER THIRTEEN

AFTER A TASTY LATE LUNCH OF

egg and lettuce sandwiches pre-prepared by Jenny,
washed down with a strong brew of bush tea, it
was midafternoon by the time they drove to the
base of Uluru.

'Over to you, Mike,' said Len, as they began their

walk. Oz had volunteered to stay at the campsite and keep an eye on Houdini with a warning from Len that the buck had been given his name for good reason. Frank was happily fast asleep, enjoying the rocking motion of Bindi's stride.

Mike explained that, as Anangu, he was a keeper of the Uluru–Kata Tjuta National Park within which Uluru stood. He asked that they stayed on the designated paths. 'So many people come here year after year and each footprint in the sand may last many weeks, and desert plants are sensitive to disturbance. Walking off-track risks the spread of weed seeds as well as the collapse of underground burrows.'

They began a meandering journey through acacia woodlands and grassed claypans. Bindi could see up close the snake-like grooves at the base of the rock, the crevasses and multicoloured layers of sandstone. It was beautiful.

'When are we going to climb it?' asked Damian. 'I bet I could give you two old farts a run for your money. Up for a race?'

Mike opened his mouth to speak but Bindi got there first. 'In the old times lots of significant ceremonies took place on Uluru, and now the land is sacred. It's a very special place culturally,' she explained.

'So?' asked Damian.

'So it's considered disrespectful to climb the rock,' added Len.

'That's stupid!' said Damian. 'I know heaps of people in the States who have climbed it.'

'Firstly,' said Mike, 'we ask visitors not to climb Uluru because of its spiritual significance as the traditional route of the ancestral *Mala* men on their arrival at Uluru. We prefer that visitors explore Uluru through our guided walks,' said Mike. 'And secondly, I take offence at being called an old fart.'

'Whatever,' sighed Damian.

Bindi felt for Damian. She could tell he was desperately trying to prove himself but felt constantly thwarted by the adults around him.

'You are free to climb Uluru, Damian, but I'd prefer you didn't. And you're my guest here and tonight we're Mike and Oz's guests,' concluded Len.

Damian scuffed his sneaker in the dust. 'All right, all right,' he muttered.

'Hey, look!' whispered Bindi, as she pointed to a small furry animal that looked like a hare. 'Is that a rufous hare wallaby?'

The little wallaby had thick brown fur with darker paws, feet and tail, and large black beady eyes. He was snuffling around on all fours, almost completely camouflaged by the long spinifex grass.

'It sure is. Thanks to the hard work of the Anangu and Uluru–Kata Tjuta National Park rangers, the rufous hare wallaby – also called the mala – is thriving in this area,' said Len. 'They are critically endangered, but in 2005 they introduced a special enclosure to the park to boost numbers.'

'And a recent survey has shown that the numbers are growing by about 100 per year,' added Mike. 'It's good to have some positive news about this wallaby and its future.'

They were mainly quiet as they continued the walk. Mike stopped every now and then to point something out. There was something about being dwarfed by a rock so huge and impressive, and rising out of nothing, that turned their thoughts inward.

It was nearly dark by the time they got back to the campsite. Oz had a fire going and had made them a hearty beef stew, which they all quickly polished off after the afternoon's exercise. The light was changing yet again with the radiant sunset in its last stages.

Len handed Bindi and Damian each a swag from the back of the ute.

'What's this?' asked Damian. 'Where are the tents?'

'We'll be sleeping under the stars tonight,' explained Len, cheerfully. 'A swag is like a sleeping bag, mattress and tent all rolled into one.'

'What about wild animals?' asked Damian, looking around nervously at the open and seemingly endless land surrounding them. 'Dingoes?'

'Good point,' said Len with a smile. 'How about you take first watch?'

'He's just teasing you,' said Bindi, giving Damian a friendly nudge.

'The fire will keep any animals away, and there's really nothing to worry about out here,' said Oz with a chuckle.

Bindi used the clean billycan to warm up some formula for Frank. Once she had poured the warm drink into a bottle, Bindi and the joey cuddled up inside the swag. She lay on her back and gazed up at the stars while Frank guzzled happily. 'You never see stars like this in the city,' said Bindi.

'Night, kids,' said Len. 'Big day tomorrow.'

Damian grunted as he shifted position, trying to get comfortable inside his swag.

Moments later they had all drifted off to sleep.

Bindi woke to Frank stirring in her arms. 'What's up, little guy?' she asked him.

His response was a quiet snuffling before resettling himself inside his pouch. He had managed to wiggle around so that he was cuddled up in the cradle of Bindi's neck. 'You're like a built-in hot water bottle keeping me warm,' whispered Bindi.

She had just closed her eyes when she realised there was another noise coming from near the campsite. Bindi sat up and peered around in the moonlight.

Bindi noticed that Damian's swag was empty

and guessed that it was his figure she could see leaving the campsite. She wondered if she should wake Len but decided against it, imagining how annoyed Damian would be if he was only going to use the toilet and they all came traipsing after him.

'What should I do, Frank?' she asked.

Frank gave no response. He was too busy worrying that his comfy and warm sleep was coming to an abrupt end. He objected with a few snorts, but Bindi had made up her mind.

She quickly wrapped her sling around her waist and shoulders and secured Frank before putting on her socks and shoes. It was easy to follow Damian and she noticed that he too was fully dressed and wearing shoes. After they'd been walking for ten minutes Bindi grew concerned. They were heading towards Uluru, the rock looming above them as they drew closer and closer.

Suddenly it dawned on Bindi what Damian planned to do. He was going to climb Uluru!

CHAPTER FOURTEEN

BINDI NEEDED TO CATCH UP WITH Damian. The ground was rocky and uneven and, in the moonlight, it was difficult to see where to place her feet. She clutched the sling protectively, worried about falling with Frank in her arms.

'Damian!' called Bindi, as she slowly closed the gap between them. 'Wait!'

Damian swung around in surprise. 'What do you want, nosey parker?' he asked, glaring at Bindi defiantly.

'I hope you're not going to do what I think you're going to do,' said Bindi, as she finally caught up to him.

'What's it to you?' he challenged.

'Aside from upsetting Mike, Oz and Len, it's dangerous. The rock is steep and slippery and it's night-time, you won't be able to see well enough. People have died climbing the rock!' cried Bindi.

Damian shrugged her off and kept walking. 'I'm so sick of everyone telling me what to do,' stormed Damian, 'and treating me like a little kid!'

'Stop acting like one then!' shouted Bindi, following behind him.

Damian swung around in surprise.

'You've done nothing but whinge since you arrived in Australia,' said Bindi. 'It's an amazing place but you just seem to want to ruin everything for everyone around you. Can you try to think of someone other than yourself? Can you imagine how upset your mum and Katie would be if anything happened to you?'

'They'd probably cheer!' sneered Damian.

'You know that's not true. They're really worried about you,' argued Bindi.

Damian nodded. 'Okay, so they're worried about me. Well, I just want to have some fun. Do cool stuff. I'm sick of everyone wanting to talk about my feelings all the time and wrap me in cotton wool.' Damian turned away and began to jog. 'Do me a favour and just leave me alone!'

Bindi tried to keep up but, in her haste, she stepped on a loose rock and almost fell. She was worried about Frank getting hurt so she decided to go back to the campsite and tell Len what had happened. Just as she made up her mind, she heard a deep male voice in the dark.

'Where do you think you're going?' Len loomed up in front of Damian, blocking his way.

'To do something fun!' huffed Damian.

Len shook his head in dismay. 'You just don't get it, do you? It's not a competition. It's not about conquering the rock by climbing it. It's about listening to the rock, being open to what it has to tell you. That's what being at one with nature is all about.'

'What do you think the rock has to tell *me*?' snapped Damian.

'That you're not as tough as you would have us believe?' suggested Len.

Damian glared at Len. He held out his hands in frustration and yelled out into the night. 'AAAHHH!'

Bindi watched as Len too took a deep breath and yelled. 'AAAHHH!' The sound echoed into the dark night sky.

Len turned to Bindi. 'Shall we all do one?'

'This is dumb,' said Damian.

'AAAHHH!' yelled Bindi, before cracking up laughing.

Len joined in so that their cries echoed all around them.

'That sounds pretty spooky,' smirked Damian, before joining the chorus. 'AAAHHH!'

Soon they had screamed themselves hoarse and collapsed on the ground, laughing.

'That felt weird but good!' said Bindi. 'Although I don't think Frank's very impressed.'

The squirming bundle on her chest wriggled further down into the sling.

'I know you lost your dad,' Len said to Damian. 'I understand it must be really difficult and painful, especially as you're at an age where you would be looking to your dad for lots of things.'

Damian shrugged.

'In Aboriginal culture,' Len continued, 'they have rites of passage that boys your age must undergo in order to be accepted as men in the tribe. They pass a series of physical and mental tests in order to strengthen them for the rigours of what it means to be a man.'

'What do they do?' asked Damian.

'It's all secret to us outsiders. And, unfortunately, our Western society doesn't really have anything like that for young men. It's a shame.' He scrutinised Damian. 'So I understand that you must feel a little lost.'

'What would you know, anyway?' Damian muttered after a pause.

'The three of us have something in common,' said Len, as he put an arm around Bindi. 'We all lost our fathers at a young age. So, Damian, I do know a little about what you're going through.'

Damian looked at the ground and didn't say anything.

'Thing is, kiddo, you are going to have to step

up and become the man of the house.' Len tapped Damian on the chest with his index finger. 'Find the warrior inside you. Your dad was a warrior. He was brave. You need to be brave and be there for your mum and sister. Do you understand?'

Damian didn't look up but his head gave the tiniest of nods.

'Don't forget that people care about you. Bindi and I can help if you'll let us,' said Len. He leaned forward and his hand brushed Damian's ear.

'Don't tell me you're going to do a corny magic trick to try and win me over,' groaned Damian.

'No, I was going to tell you you've got half the national park growing out of your head,' said Len, pulling a small leafy twig from Damian's hair. He gave Damian a clap on the back. 'Come on, let's hit the hay. I need my beauty sleep. I'm an old fart, remember?'

Damian smirked. He looked back at the sheer rock face before turning to the others with a nod. Len led the way back to camp with Bindi and Damian following in single file.

CHAPTER FIFTEEN

JUST AFTER SUNRISE THE NEXT
morning, the group had packed up the campsite
and loaded the ute. Len allowed Houdini to stretch
his legs before loading him onto the back of the
ute. They waved goodbye to Mike and Oz, and
headed off.

As the only vehicle on the highway at such an early hour, it felt like they had the view of Uluru all to themselves. In the orange light of dawn, the rock appeared even larger than it had the day before.

'It's kind of eerie,' yelled Damian, his head stuck out the window. 'No matter where I'm looking it's as if the rock is watching me.'

'Maybe it's watching *over* you?' suggested Bindi.

Frank peeped his head out from the pouch and looked up at Bindi and Damian.

'Guys, look!' whispered Bindi. 'That's the first time Frank has stuck his head out of the pouch.'

'Your little boy is growing up,' smiled Len.

'He's hungry,' said Bindi, as she reached over for the bottle she had prepared for the car trip. 'Would you like to try feeding him?' she asked Damian.

Damian pulled a face. 'He's so tiny, I'm scared I'll hurt him.'

'You'll be fine,' Bindi said reassuringly, handing him the bottle.

'Come on,' said Len, 'time to step up.'

Damian took the little bundle from Bindi and placed Frank gingerly in his lap. He held the bottle at the angle he had seen Bindi hold it. 'Here you go, Frankie,' he said in a low voice. 'Breakfast time.'

The joey needed little encouragement and began sucking noisily on the teat. Damian gazed down at Frank's furry face and cute whiskers, and grimaced as Frank's tiny claws sank into Damian's jeans. The joey's wet, black nose twitched and his oversized ears flopped as he drank contentedly. In an instant Damian was smitten with his charge.

Bindi glanced at Len, and they shared a smile.

By late morning they pulled into the spot Len had picked out to release Houdini.

'The Watarrka National Park is nearby,' Len pointed out. 'It's a great spot for roos, and I've been watching one mob in particular for some time.'

'It's beautiful here,' breathed Bindi. 'I think Houdini will be very happy.'

They looked out over the scrub, spinifex grasses and rugged ranges beyond.

'The way a roo mob works is that there is only one dominant male. It will only work for Houdini if he is submissive to the head of the pack. If not, he won't be accepted and could possibly be hurt,' Len explained. 'Fingers crossed.'

He unlocked the enclosure and coaxed Houdini outside with the promise of food. Human contact with the young buck had been deliberately limited over the past few months in order to prepare Houdini for life in the wild. It had been hard for Len and Jenny to distance themselves from a roo they had reared since he was only a few weeks old, but they wanted the best possible future for Houdini. Too many people took in joeys without a thought for what they would do with them once fully grown.

'Come on, old friend,' said Len. 'This is your new playground.'

Houdini hesitantly hopped a few metres away from the ute and sniffed the air. It was only now, seeing him out of captivity, that Bindi realised just how large he was. Red male kangaroos can grow up to three metres, and Houdini was close to that size. He stood up on his hind legs and towered above them.

'Did you know that red kangaroos can jump up to eight metres far and three metres high?' asked Len.

'Those hind legs sure look powerful,' said Bindi.

'Another interesting fact about kangaroos is that they're excellent swimmers,' said Len. 'Their legs can't move independently of one another on land, so they hop. But in the water, when they are kicking, they can move their legs independently.'

'You're a walking kangaroo encyclopedia, aren't you?' Damian said with a smile.

'I like to think so,' chuckled Len.

They watched Houdini take a few more jumps away from them.

'See you then, old mate. Off you go!' encouraged Len.

'Bye, Houdini,' said Bindi, as she gave the young buck a wave. Damian held up a hand to say goodbye to the kangaroo.

And all too soon he was off.

'His final act of escapology!' said Len.

Bindi noticed that Len's eyes were moist. 'Are you okay, Len?' she asked, putting a hand on his arm.

'I'm not about to start blubbering if that's what you're worried about,' said Len. 'But I am a little emotional. It's like being a father and watching your child on their first day of school. You're proud as punch but a part of you doesn't want to let go.'

'He won't forget you,' said Bindi.

'Maybe he will, maybe he won't,' said Len. 'Let's

just hope he has a long life. I'd like to follow at a distance and see how he goes once he finds the mob.'

Damian and Bindi nodded. They also wanted to make sure Houdini got on okay with his new family.

They spent the next hour exploring part of Watarrka National Park and waiting to see if Houdini would approach the mob. The park was best known as the home of Kings Canyon, a mighty chasm which descends into the earth to a depth of 270 metres. The canyon's sheer rock face soared high above the dense forests of palms, ferns and cycads.

'Look!' Len called the kids over and pointed. They were standing high on a cliff that over-looked the mob of red kangaroos. Bindi counted roughly fifteen kangaroos of various sizes grazing leisurely.

'The dominant male is issuing Houdini a challenge,' said Len.

They watched as the huge kangaroo adopted a higher standing posture and grasped Houdini's neck with its forepaw. They proceeded to paw at each other's heads, shoulders and chests.

'They're going to box!' said Bindi. She couldn't help but feel anxious about Houdini and how he would interact with other wild kangaroos.

The battle continued with Houdini and the head of the mob locking forearms and wrestling as they pushed and kicked at each other.

'Go, Houdini!' cheered Damian.

Len shook his head. 'No, Houdini won't win this fight. He's still too young. He needs to realise the only way to join this family is if he submits.'

The struggle continued until Houdini finally broke off and retreated. It was over as quickly as it had begun. The male leader went back to grazing, and Houdini began to graze a few metres away.

'Attaboy!' Len punched the air with his fist.

'Phew!' sighed Bindi. 'That was stressful.'

'*That* was cool,' said Damian.

'I'm going to give Jenny a call to give her the good news,' said Len, and pulled his phone out of his pocket.

He turned it on and was alerted to six missed calls from home. As he listened to a message, Bindi and Damian watched Len's smile quickly vanish from his face.

'What is it?' asked Damian.

'Jenny got a call from a friend of hers who overheard a roo hunter bragging in the pub last night about how many roos he's killed,' said Len in a strangled voice. 'He also said he's going to be hunting in this area tonight.'

CHAPTER SIXTEEN

'HOUDINI!' CRIED BINDI.

'Not to mention his new family,' said Len, as he placed the phone back in his pocket. 'They'll be wiped out, just like that.'

'But this is a national park,' Bindi pointed out. 'Surely the roos are protected?'

'The border to the national park ends near here, and from then on it's farmland. It would be open season for a hunter,' Len explained.

'Hunting's really common in the States,' said Damian. 'Nobody bats an eyelid.'

'All those months of rehabilitating Houdini,' muttered Len, shaking his head, 'and for what?'

'We have to stop him!' said Bindi.

Damian turned to her. 'What difference will it make if we stop him tonight?'

'We have to try!' cried Bindi. 'Right, Len? Len?' She grabbed Len by the hand in an effort to gain his attention. 'My dad was a Wildlife Warrior. He spent his life fighting for the rights of animals because he believed in a cause. He was a soldier of one against incredible odds, and he never gave up.'

'But hunters will just come back the next night or the ones after that,' argued Damian.

'Maybe we can get through to him,' pleaded Bindi. 'It's worth a shot, isn't it?'

'Shot?' said Len in a dazed voice. 'I chose this area because, as far as I knew, they never shoot around here.'

'Damian, you have to help me!' cried Bindi.

'I don't know, Bindi,' Damian's voice trailed off uncertainly.

'What about Frank?' asked Bindi, pointing to the little joey in Damian's arms. 'Don't you want him to have a future?'

'What's the point?' asked Damian. 'Everything dies at some point anyway.'

'That's no reason not to try to stop a cruel practice. Roos are shot at random in the dead of the night.

Females are often killed with the joeys left to starve to death.' Bindi was getting more and more worked up. 'Each year thousands of joeys die this way. Some of the females are too small to get enough meat or hide off so they're left behind, the roos are hung up off the side of a truck.'

'We can't stop an entire industry, Bindi,' reasoned Damian.

'No, but we can maybe stop one hunter *this* time,' pleaded Bindi. 'Think about Frank and his future!'

Damian looked down at Frank, whose head was sticking out of the pouch. He could feel his blood boil at the thought of anyone trying to hurt the joey. Damian looked up and met Bindi's eyes. 'What did you have in mind?' he asked.

Once Len had got over his shock, he brought the others up to speed about what to expect from a roo hunter.

'He'll be driving a special four-wheel drive, a little like my ute but bigger. There will be a special cab-type tray on the back. On it will be a welded rack, custom-built and fitted with steel pins on which to hang the roos.'

'It makes me shudder just to picture it,' said Bindi, wincing.

Len absentmindedly picked up an apple and held it in one hand as he talked. 'He'll remain in his car and use a powerful spotlight he can operate from inside the cab. He'll wind his window down on the driver's side and use a rifle with a scope to make his hit.'

'But kangaroos can hop fast, can't they?' asked Damian. 'Could they out-hop the car?'

'Some of them will get away. But he'll catch them unaware at night when they'll be drowsy or asleep,' said Len bitterly. 'They're good shots, these men.'

'So what's the plan?' asked Damian.

'I think our only hope is if we scare this mob deep into a canyon so that he never finds them in the first place,' said Len. 'If he has a fruitless night, he might not bother to come back all this way again.'

'And how do three people move a mob of kangaroos?' asked Damian.

'Good question!' said Len with a rueful expression.

CHAPTER SEVENTEEN

DAMIAN, BINDI AND LEN SPENT
what was left of the day painstakingly rounding
up the mob of red kangaroos by making as
much noise as they could. Damian and Bindi
banged billycans with spoons, Len drove the ute
and honked the horn while Frank sat in the

passenger seat wondering what all the fuss was about.

By late afternoon they'd managed to move the mob away from the road and further into the bush where they were less visible in the long spinifex grass, hidden by low trees and rocky outcrops.

'Let's hope that's far enough,' said Len, as the last of the daylight faded and dusk approached.

'What do we do now?' asked Bindi. She was covered in dust and scratches from head to toe, and although she was exhausted, Bindi couldn't keep still.

'We wait,' said Len.

Time seemed to crawl as the sun slowly set over the desert plains. It was their most beautiful sunset yet but none of them could really appreciate it. The light slowly petered out over the green grasses, blooming wildflowers and arching mulga branches; the warm tones replaced by the blue and grey tints of dusk.

From their vantage point on top of one of the gorges, Bindi and Damian anxiously watched the road in the distance for signs of a vehicle. Len stood near them, juggling apples.

'Why are you doing that?' asked Damian, bewildered.

'I often juggle when I'm nervous,' said Len. 'It gives my hands something to do and takes my mind off my worries. All I have to do is think about three balls and how to keep them in the air. It keeps things pretty simple.'

'What made you start doing magic?' asked Bindi.

'My dad bought me a magic set just before he died. We never got a chance to use it together,' said Len with a sad smile, continuing to juggle. 'It seemed like a way of being closer to him, and I like that it cheers people up. There weren't many smiles around our house for a while back then.'

'You're really good, you know,' said Damian.

'Thanks, mate,' chuckled Len. 'That's high praise coming from you.'

Damian blushed and nodded. It was true.

'Car!' cried Bindi, pointing to a set of headlights on the horizon.

Len dropped the apples one by one, and they fell hard onto the rock floor with a series of squelchy thuds.

'It could be any car,' said Damian, though he didn't sound hopeful.

They crouched down and watched as the head-lights grew brighter. The roar of the engine grew louder and soon the car was parallel to where they sat. Even in the dim light it was obvious that the car was a four-wheel drive that carried a wire cab on its back.

'This looks like our hunter,' said Len grimly.

They watched as the four-wheel drive slowed down and pulled off the road about fifty metres in front of them. Then it slowed to a halt.

'What's he doing?' whispered Damian.

'Waiting until it's completely dark,' said Len. 'Roo hunters often get to the site early so they can find it in the light, and also because it's dangerous driving on these roads at night. It's easy to hit a roo and have a bad accident.'

They sat in silence as the light faded and night

was well and truly upon them. Bindi tried to keep busy by giving Frank a feed, then settling him back into his pouch against her chest so that he could sleep comfortably. She felt even more protective of him than ever.

At nine o'clock the engine started up and the headlights came on. This time a large and powerful spotlight attached to the car's roof rack lit up in front of the four-wheel drive. As the vehicle slowly made its way over the uneven desert floor, the spotlight swept eerily over the grasses and trees.

'This is it, folks,' said Len tensely.

They watched as the car made its way in large circles around the more open ground, searching for its prey.

'He's got to give up soon,' said Bindi.

'I have a feeling he's a determined fella,' said Len. 'He won't want to go back to the pub. He probably bragged so much, he'll resist returning without a trophy or two.'

'You're wrong!' said Damian excitedly. He pointed as the car slowed to a stop.

They waited with bated breath as the vehicle remained stationary with the engine still running.

'Go home!' whispered Bindi.

Then, with a surge of power, the engine revved louder and louder. The car skidded off at a faster speed and headed deep into the bush. With a sickening feeling, Bindi realised that he wasn't going to give up. He was going to find their roo mob.

'No magic trick can save us now,' said Damian grimly.

CHAPTER EIGHTEEN

THE SPOTLIGHT DREW CLOSER and closer, sweeping the ground beneath them with its high beam. Len made his way over to the other side of the rock to get a better view.

'I've got an idea,' said Bindi, turning to Damian.

'What if we appeal to him? Flag down the car and try to talk to him?'

Damian's eyes grew wide. 'He's not going to care what two kids have to say!'

'He might,' said Bindi. 'He might have kids of his own.'

'I could fight him,' Damian suggested with a slightly hysterical laugh.

Bindi looked horrified. 'Force isn't the way, Damian.' Bindi secured the straps on Frank's sling and looked at Damian. 'Are you in?'

Damian nodded.

Bindi checked to see if Len's back was still turned. 'Quick, let's go before Len tries to stop us,' she whispered. Bindi began to pick her way down the rocks while Damian shone his torch to light their way.

They had almost reached level ground by the

time Len realised they had gone. 'Bindi!' he called down to them. 'Damian, get back here! This is dangerous!' He watched helplessly as the kids made their way closer to the four-wheel drive.

Bindi and Damian raced towards the spotlight, and waved madly to try to get the driver's attention. Damian ran ahead and yelled out to the driver to stop just as the spotlight caught him in its beam.

The LandCruiser slowed to a stop. A man wearing a baseball cap stuck his head out of the driver's window and yelled at Damian. 'What are you doing out here in the middle of nowhere?'

'Wait!' cried Damian as he approached the vehicle.

'Thank you for stopping,' Bindi panted, after catching up to them. She held out her hand to introduce herself. 'I'm Bindi Irwin, and this is Damian Paterson.'

The driver ignored her hand and scowled. 'What are you kids up to?'

'We know you've come out here to hunt kangaroos, and we wanted to ask you not to.' Bindi couldn't help but notice the rifle lying across the driver's lap.

The driver laughed and shook his head. 'Is there a hidden camera somewhere?'

'This isn't a joke,' said Damian, using the toughest voice he could muster. 'We want you to think about the joeys that get left behind when their mums and dads get killed. Most of them will starve to death.'

Bindi unwrapped her sling and pulled out Frank, who opened his eyes and looked at the driver. Frank blinked a few times and stretched out a tiny paw by way of introduction.

'This is Frank. He was orphaned like thousands of other joeys every year. If it wasn't for volunteers who devote countless hours to hand-rearing the joeys, he would have had no chance of survival,' said Bindi.

'What's it to me?' growled the driver. He looked to be in his late forties and, by the size of his hands on the wheel, Bindi could tell he was a strong man.

'You don't have to do this,' she said. 'The kangaroo is an icon and part of our cultural heritage – a wild animal which should be treated with the utmost respect.'

'I've heard about enough from you lot,' snarled the driver. 'I have work to do. Clear off!'

'Do you have kids?' asked Damian.

The driver looked angry. 'What's it to you?'

'Do they know that sometimes roos take hours to die on the back of your truck?' asked Damian.

The driver was now most definitely angry. 'I do have kids and they know that my job puts food on the table.' He fingered the trigger on his rifle. 'Get out of my way, kid, before you get hurt.'

He stepped hard on the accelerator, and the LandCruiser took off. It skidded in the loose gravel and dirt, sending a spray of stones and dust right into Bindi and Damian's faces.

'Aahh!' cried Damian, as he tried to shield his eyes.

Bindi swung around to protect Frank, and bent over in the dirt.

'Are you okay, Bindi?' asked Damian.

Bindi nodded and wiped the dust from her face.

'I think so.' She checked on Frank. He had wisely buried his head inside her top and seemed fine.

'Are you kids insane?' They turned to see Len standing right behind them with his hands on his hips.

'He needs to be stopped!' Damian cried. He was furious and past caring what any adult thought. 'He's not going to get away with it!' he yelled, and before Bindi or Len could do or say anything, Damian sprinted after the car at full speed.

CHAPTER NINETEEN

DAMIAN FELT VERY FOCUSED and clear for the first time in a long time. All he had to think about was where to put his feet and to move his body as fast as he could in the direction of the lights. He couldn't run as fast as the car but he was more agile. He was able to dodge rocks and

and bushes more easily. He felt some of the gap between him and his target closing.

'Come on,' he muttered to himself. 'You can do this.'

He could hear the sound of his laboured breathing, the sound of the car and the noise the wheels made as they bore down on the sand and loose stones. He remembered that he used to like to run and he remembered that he was good at it. With each step his legs began to scream, his muscles unused to the effort. His lungs burned and he thought about giving up.

Damian pictured the sight of Houdini's new mob grazing in their natural habitat, and how peaceful they had looked. He pictured Frank's comical oversized ears and the way he freaked out if you took too long to give him his bottle. Damian clenched his fists and dug deep inside himself for the strength to keep running.

'Run, Houdini!' he shouted into the night sky. 'Get away!'

He allowed his mind to shut down and felt his body take over. He ran. It was all he could do. And then he saw his chance. The LandCruiser needed to swing right to get around a clump of trees. Damian calculated that if he jumped the boulder in front of him, he would land parallel to the car.

He bounded onto the rock and, without pause to consider, he jumped onto the bare earth on the other side. His landing, however, wasn't as perfect, and he fell onto one knee. He regained his balance and saw from the corner of his eye that the car was pulling up alongside of him.

'Stop!' he yelled to the driver. Out of the corner

of his eye Damian could see the driver's profile and the insidious rifle lying on its rest, the barrel seemingly pointed at him.

The car didn't seem to be slowing down. In fact, it was speeding up! Inch by inch the LandCruiser was gaining ground. Damian summoned all the strength he had and kept running.

But it was too late, he just couldn't keep up. The LandCruiser pulled ahead, and as Damian cried out in exasperation, his ankle gave way under a loose rock and he fell. He landed hard on the ground, rolled and tasted the dirt and gravel as his head hit the ground. Dust flew all around him, and he could see the particles of desert, lit up like stars, as they floated down upon him. Then there was darkness.

Bindi and Len found Damian lying on his back, looking up at the night sky.

'Yikes,' said Len, when he saw the grazes on Damian's arms and legs. 'You've lost some skin there, son.'

'I couldn't stop him,' Damian said weakly. 'I tried. I *really* tried but it wasn't enough.'

'You did your best,' said Bindi. 'That's all anyone can ask of you.'

'What about Houdini and the roos?' said Damian.'

'You could have got yourself seriously hurt, mate,' said Len. 'How would I have explained that to your mother?'

Bindi knelt down next to Damian. 'I'm just glad that you're okay.' She studied him. '*Are* you okay?'

Damian nodded and grimaced. 'I will be, thanks for asking.'

Len held out a hand and pulled Damian up to stand.

'I've been listening for the gunshots but I haven't heard any,' said Damian. He winced as he tried to bear weight on his right leg.

'I don't think we'll be hearing any shots tonight, after all,' said Len with a wink.

'Why do I get the feeling you know something that we don't?' asked Bindi.

'Well,' said Len, 'we have Damian to thank, actually.'

'We do?' asked Damian, looking surprised.

'You gave me the idea when you said we needed a magic trick to stop the hunter. I followed you to the LandCruiser and, while you were appealing to his better nature, I put some sugar in his tank while removing his spare can of fuel,' laughed Len.

'I don't believe it!' said Damian, incredulous.

'He won't get far,' said Len, 'and he'll have lots of time to reflect on his choice of vocation.' Len gazed out into the blackness before adding, 'It's a long walk to the nearest town.'

Bindi giggled. 'Now that's a magic trick I wish I had seen!'

Len chuckled. 'I doubt your mothers would approve, so maybe this can be our little secret?' He tapped the side of his nose conspiratorially.

Damian looked at Bindi. They both smiled and repeated the gesture.

'You've got yourself a deal,' said Damian.

CHAPTER TWENTY

BINDI FELT SAD TO BE LEAVING

Uluru but she was also excited about seeing her mum and Robert again. She leapt out of the ute even before Len had brought the vehicle to a stop when they pulled up at the kangaroo sanctuary.

'Mum! Robert!' cried Bindi, racing past the gate and into the centre.

Terri and Robert were helping Katie feed a joey while Amanda stood by, nursing a little bundle of her own.

Katie was the first to see Bindi bounding over. 'Bindi, look, I'm feeding a joey!' she announced proudly.

'Good for you, Katie!' Bindi was impressed. In only three days the Patersons had become experienced kangaroo carers.

'Where's Damian?' asked Amanda. She was anxious to see how her son was coping after his time in the outback.

Damian walked in carrying Frank in the sling. 'Hi everyone,' he said with a wave.

'Damian,' sighed Amanda, relieved to see he

was in good spirits. She walked over to greet her son and gave him a hug, though it was slightly difficult as they both had joey bumps to negotiate.

'We missed you,' Amanda said softly.

'I missed you too,' said Damian, with no hint of sarcasm. 'Mum, for what it's worth, I'm sorry I've been a jerk.'

Amanda's eyes grew moist. 'That's okay. You've had so much to deal with.'

Damian shrugged. 'So have you and Katie, but you guys weren't jerks.' He struggled to find the right words. 'I just didn't know where to begin so it was easier to try and block it all out.'

Amanda nodded. 'I understand.'

Damian reached out a hand to stroke his mother's hair, just behind her ear.

'Oh, honey,' she said, touched by the gesture.

Damian withdrew his hand and held up a shiny one-dollar coin. 'Now how did that get there?' he asked with a smile.

Amanda giggled. 'Looks like someone's been teaching you a few of their tricks.'

Damian nodded. He looked over at Len giving Jenny a hug. 'He's all right, even if he's completely bonkers!'

KANGAROOS

Australia Zoo is passionate about spreading awareness of the plight faced by one of our national icons – the kangaroo. The commercial killing of kangaroos is the largest terrestrial wildlife slaughter in the world. Because the kill quotas outnumber the reproductive rate of kangaroos, most industry experts expect the red kangaroo to disappear within the next ten years, unless the shooting is stopped.

Russia, once the largest importer of kangaroo meat, banned the importation of kangaroo products in 2010. The reasons given for this were the consistent contamination of the kangaroo products, and concern about the inhumane treatment of joeys. This recent ban on kangaroo meat may help the fight to increase our kangaroo populations.

To find out more about the protection of
Australian wildlife, please visit:

www.wildlifewarriors.org.au